Bremer Lagerhaus

Bremen - The World Port

Bremer Lagerhaus

Bremen - The World Port

ISBN/EAN: 9783954274055
Erscheinungsjahr: 2014
Erscheinungsort: Bremen, Deutschland

© maritimepress in Europäischer Hochschulverlag GmbH & Co. KG, Fahrenheitstr. 1, 28359 Bremen. Alle Rechte beim Verlag und bei den jeweiligen Lizenzgebern.

www.maritimepress.de | office@maritimepress.de

Bei diesem Titel handelt es sich um den Nachdruck eines historischen, lange vergriffenen Buches. Da elektronische Druckvorlagen für diese Titel nicht existieren, musste auf alte Vorlagen zurückgegriffen werden. Hieraus zwangsläufig resultierende Qualitätsverluste bitten wir zu entschuldigen.

Bremer Lagerhaus

Bremen - The World Port

BREMEN THE WORLD PORT

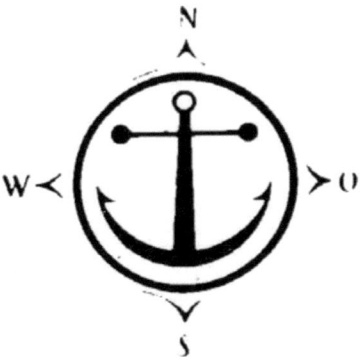

(50 miles from the mouth of the Weser).

BREMEN THE WORLD PORT

Bremen holds a unique position among the German seaports. It is the German port which allows ocean-going vessels to advance farthest inland. Bremen is a reservoir for such valuable imports as cotton, tobacco, grain, and rice, as well as an export place for Germany's high-class industrial products. The Port of Bremen is, above all, a railway port. 85 per cent. of its overseas traffic is received from or transferred to the railways. Situation and equipment of the harbors of Bremen guarantee that the cargo is transferred with

Speed, Caution, Safety and Economy

The Docks of Bremen are lined with wide quays and warehouses covering a total area of 479 000 ☐ yards.

Situation   Bremen is situated about 50 miles from the entrance to the Weser Estuary, i. e. more than 31 miles farther south than Hamburg and more than 18,8 miles farther to the south than Emden. Both the Outer and the Lower Weser have been developed in a model way as a shipping lane for large ocean-going craft. Even in the severest winter both sections remain open to shipping. Ocean steamers of the present standard size are able to navigate the Weser from its mouth to Bremen City on one tide. The Weser Estuary has the best fairway among the German shipping lanes to the sea. Bremerhaven, the passenger port of Bremen, is accessible to the largest express steamers, independent of the tides.

Freeport II, 1,1 miles long, accommodating 84 large freighters at one time.

The docks of Bremen City are located at the outskirts of the town. They comprise 13 basins. Most of these are open river docks while some are fitted with locks. The latter docks afford favorable sites for large industrial establishments and are equipped for the transfer of bulk goods such as potash, coal, and ores. The tidal docks on the open river (the tide runs in as far as the "Bremer Wehr" [barrage] above the city) are serving the multifarious requirements of the European and transoceanic freight traffic. They also include within their precincts shipyards, grain silos, and a number of industrial plants (oil and flour mills, the "Hag" Coffee Works, and others). In her daughter-town, Bremerhaven, Bremen owns another large port with 7 mooring basins and, on the open river, an extensive passenger pier with a railway station. Here the liners of the type of the "Bremen", the "Europa", and the "Columbus" are accommodated. In addition, the docks of Bremerhaven serve for the transshipment of valuable bulk goods.

The Docks

Owing to the particular character of Bremen as a railway port, the harbor basins have a relatively small width. All along the extensive docks lie capacious

Being intended for the direct transfer of freight from ship to railway, the docks of Bremen have far-flung basins surrounded by stone quays and equipped with extensive railway tracks, sheds and warehouses.

In the dry-docks of Bremen and Bremerhaven ships of all sizes may be thoroughly overhauled and repaired.

space of 437,000 □ yards, the storage sheds and warehouses a floor space of 479,000 □ yards. 278 shore cranes capable of lifting from 1,5 to 10 tons, 21 warehouse cranes, and 120 warehouse elevators and winches serve to handle cargo.

Rapid Transfer

In the docks serving in-and out-bound shipping the quays are equipped with double and treble railway tracks, those of the newest sections with four tracks. On the land-side of the quay sheds lie two more tracks, beyond which are the roadway and the public warehouses with their own sidings. This system ensures the d i r e c t t r a n s f e r of a maximum volume of merchandise from ship to railway and vice versa, as well as the r a p i d attendance to quays and sheds. At the ends of the different freight sidings are large groups of marshalling tracks which effect a fast exchange of cars on the loading tracks between working hours. The previous distribution of the cars is done within the dock limits at the shunting depots which cover an area of from 2 to 2,5 miles. There the freight trains are shunted from

quays equipped with a network of railway sidings, cranes, elevators, and winches, sheds and warehouses, and all further appliances required for the transshipment of valuable freight between ship and railway or ship and warehouse. On an average, there are 7 miles of sidings to 1 mile of waterfront in the Bremen docks, including the industrial docks. The aggregate length of railway tracks to a total quay length of 27 miles amounts to 180 miles. The cargo sheds on the quays have a total floor

The docks of Bremen are accessible to all standard-size ships.

In the docks of Bremen 7 miles of railway tracks fall to 1 mile of quay. Two, three and four tracks, parallel to the waterfront, facilitate direct transshipment from ship to railway and vice versa.

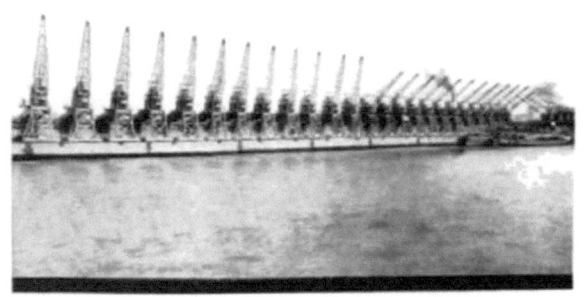

The quay of Dock II is equipped with 36 cranes of the latest type, ten of which can be set to work simultaneously on one ship. All in all, the docks are fitted with 240 shore cranes, each lifting from 1,5 to 10 tons.

the dock railway to the Reichsbahn, and vice versa, while undergoing also the customs examination without loss of time.

Between the quay sheds and the warehouses special cranes have been erected which move the merchandise directly from the sheds to the different floors of the warehouses. The latter serve not only for prolonged storage but also for the accommodation of freight remaining only a short time in port, either as transit goods or for re-exportation (transit stores).

Careful Transfer

Careful treatment of merchandise is best assured by handling it as little as possible. The more the goods are shifted in port, the greater becomes the danger of their being damaged. The longer they are on the way between the different means of transport — ship, railway, or cart —, the more easily are they exposed to injury. The Port of Bremen offers the advantage of the goods being transferred directly from railway to steamer, or vice versa. The Bremen docks are, moreover, eminently adapted for the handling of freight which has to be stored for commercial purposes before being forwarded. The transit sheds, situated directly on the quays, are fitted with wide loading platforms from which the cargo is lifted by reliable cranes across the sidings into the ship's hold. Nor are goods discharged from a ship put down on deck first, but are hauled directly out of the hold and lifted over to the loading platform. In the well-lighted and

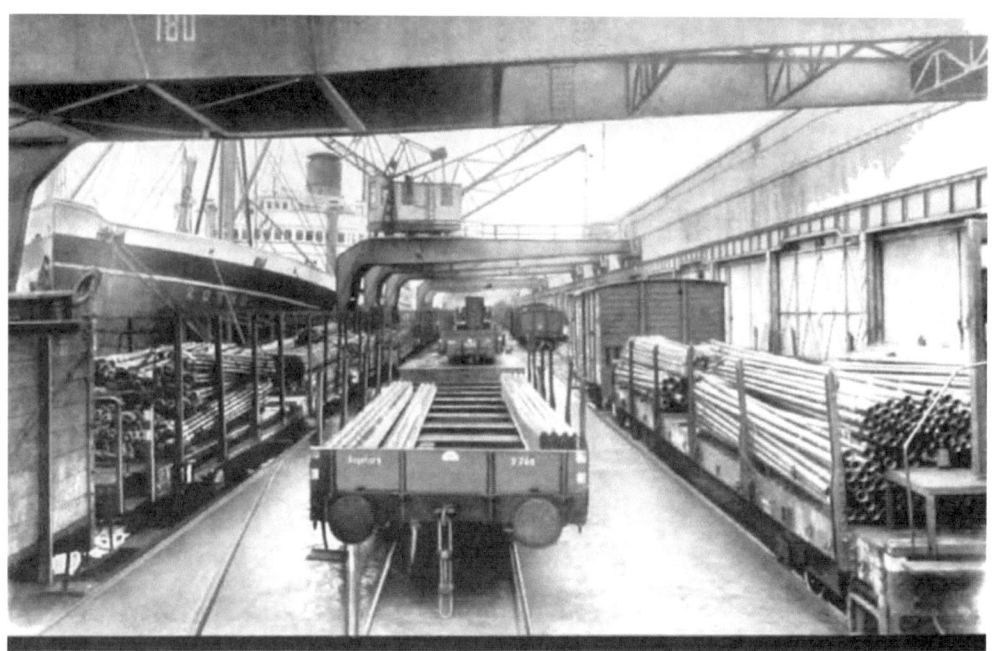

About 80 per cent. of the freight transshipped is moved from ship to rail, or vice versa. There are 180 miles of railway tracks to a useful quay length of 27 miles.

Man at the winch loading bags.

spacious sheds goods are not stacked but each parcel is accessible on the floor.

In order to provide ample light, which is necessary for the adequate treatment of the goods, about one-third of the roof space is fitted with skylights. Every provision is made also for goods that have to be warehoused in port, possibly because the owner has not yet given orders for their transfer. The public warehouses are situated directly behind the quay sheds; so the cranes can move the goods safely between the sheds and the different floors of the warehouses whenever it is required.

Floating cranes capable of lifting up to 110 tons serve to reload exceptionally weighty cargo.

Unusually extensive technical and architectural safety devices for the prevention and fighting of fire protect the goods in that direction. Considering the technical perfection of this fire control, among which the sprinkler installations in most of the sheds deserve to be mentioned, the insurance companies grant a reduction of 30 % on their premium.

Thefts rarely occur in the harbors of Bremen. During working hours special overseers are on duty. After working hours the sheds are locked, but even then the docks are patrolled by watchmen. The Harbor Board works in conjunction with the control service of the German Railway Company. The Freeport Zone is surrounded by strong railings, the gates of which are constantly guarded by customs officers.

Safe Transfer

Forwarders are entitled to demand a threefold surety with regard to the handling of merchandise in port, viz., against general injury, against damage by fire, and against theft.

Merchandise in the docks of Bremen is safeguarded against general injury because it is scarcely exposed to the influence of the weather while being transferred from railway to steamer as well as to and from the sheds. Moreover, the sheds are entirely protected against rain from all sides. The lofty structure of the sheds, and their ample ventilation are also instrumental in keeping the merchandise in good condition.

Testing the hoisting power of a pontoon crane.

A heavy locomotive boiler is shipped with the aid of a floating crane in Dock II.

11

Bagged merchandise (rice, peanuts, copra, cotton seed).

Cheap Transfer

In order to ensure an as cheap as possible operation of the harbor traffic, the Government of Bremen has leased, since the opening of the Free Port, that part of the port business which is suitable for commercial management to a warehousing company, the Bremer Lagerhaus - Gesellschaft. In a similar manner Hamburg has entrusted the management of the warehouses in the Port of Hamburg to the Hamburger Freihafen Lagerhaus - Gesellschaft, whereas the transfer traffic remained under the control of the State Board of Quays. In Luebeck the Chamber of Commerce has assumed charge of the docks. The State of Bremen shares in the revenues of the Bremer Lagerhaus-Gesellschaft. The government determines the port fees, aside from exercising a far-reaching right of control. The Lagerhausgesellschaft attends to the entire transshipment and storage business in the harbor, while the rest of the port management, especially the construction and upkeep of the docks, is in the hands of the State Deputation for Harbors and Railways. The management of the port is therefore partly in the hands of the State, and partly under joint government and private supervision. The government administration includes architectural, nautical and police matters, while the joint management is responsible for the transshipment and warehouse traffic.

The separation of the administrative from the operative management has proved very satisfactory for the State of Bremen as well as for the commercial interests of the city. Thus the merchant has obtained

In a fruit shed. Auction sale of southern fruit (Canary Island bananas, American apples, Hawaiian pineapples, oranges, etc).

Virginia tobacco is shipped to Europe in barrels.

Copper bars stacked in the foreground.

Transshipment plant for bulk goods (Röchling & Co.)

a more agile co-operator, that is, one better able to adapt himself to the prevailing market and business conditions than the government itself.

Being the most southerly situated seaport of Germany, Bremen offers the further advantage of affording the lowest railway freight rates to the interior. The preferential tariffs granted to the seaports by the German Railways thoroughly accentuate the accessibility of the hinterland. This fact should be fully appreciated, since the oversea freight rates to the Continental North Sea ports are, on the whole, independent of the location and particularly of the distance ocean-going vessels have to advance inland Bremen's excellent port facilities warrant the speedy despatch of transfer cargoes. The stay of ocean-going ships in port is shortened by the recently installed luffing cranes which load and discharge cargo in a minimum of time.

Canaries from the Harz Mts. on the way to New York

The equipment of Dock II permits the discharging of a cotton steamer with 15 000 bales within 18 hours.

View in one of the spacious cotton sheds. One-tenth of an average American cotton crop may be stored at one time in the cotton sheds of Bremen.

The Roland Flour Mill. Tower building on the Lumber and Factory Dock, around which several industries, such as flour and oil mills, the Hag Coffee Works, and others, have settled. All are directly connected with the shipping traffic.

Special Transfer-Facilities

1 The **grain elevator and grain transshipment plant** on Dock III is the largest of its kind on the European Continent. About 1 000 000 t of grain are transferred a year without exhausting the capacity of the station whose piers allow four ocean vessels to be handled at one time. The piers are equipped with suction elevators, self-acting

View of the Grain Elevator and Transhipment Station.

Pneumatic elevators suck the grain out of the hold. Four ocean steamers can be handled simultaneously at the piers of the establishment.

standard-gauge scales with sacking funnels, railway tracks with loading banks, and conveyors for the removal of grain to the respective storehouses. The station is designed for the transfer of grain arriving by steamer and offers all requisites in a completeness not met with in other plants of the kind. Beside the transfer from ship to ship customary with floating elevators, this plant enables the direct reloading of grain into railway cars on the piers, a method significant for Bremen as a railway port. It also permits the removal to the silos of grain not yet disposed of, or grain which cannot be transferred at once owing to a lack of rolling stock. The hourly output lies between 600 and 700 t. The maximum achieved up-to-date was 7400 t a day. The storage house, which is chiefly intended for the balance of shipments passing through the station, is fitted with silos and grain floors. Its function is similar to that of the quay-sheds with regard to other merchandise. This establishment is able to hold 23 000 tons and is

Conveyor belts of a total length of 3,5 miles move the potash salts from the river craft or the railway to the store, or from the store to the deep-water ship.

The Potash Station is able to handle 5000 t of potash a day. Conveyor bridges for grab operation, 72 ft. high and 98 ft. wide, shift the potash from the river craft to the ocean steamer or to the store.

now being enlarged to a capacity of 56 000 tons.
2. The **Potash Depot**, located on a basin of the Industrial Harbor, was established in 1928 and serves for the shipping of potassium salts overseas. Due to the peculiar qualities of potassium salts and the special requirements of the trade, the transfer of potash demands facilities which can only be supplied by a special plant. The depot includes a main building of 295 yards frontage. In front of this structure are three conveyor bridges, each 72 ft. high. Their hinged jibs, constructed to reach 98 ft. beyond the edge of the quay, are capable of lifting the potash from two river barges moored alongside the outside of an ocean steamer over the side and into the hold of the latter, or into the storage floors of the station. The grab takes 2.5 to 3 tons of potash at a time. Four smaller conveyors are erected beneath the main conveyor bridges, by which the potash, be it in bulk or sacked, is carried from the stores or straight from the railway to the steamer.

Chutes on which the automatically sacked potash is slid into the ship.

A system of conveyor belts of an aggregate length of 3.5 miles in the main building carries the salts from the river craft or the railway cars to the stores, and from the stores to the deepwater ships. Six large storage halls for the reception of different kinds of potassium salts are situated at the back of the main building. These stores hold 100 000 to 120 000 tons valued at 2.8 to 3 million dollars. Travelling scrapers (dredger-like transporters) scrape the hardened salt off the mounds in the storage halls to the conveyor belts. The potash is kept dry by a system of heating tubes 4.33 miles in extent. The transferring capacity of the entire plant attains 5000 tons a day while attending to two ocean steamers. In 1929, 360 000 tons of potash were transshipped at this depot.

3. **Transfer of Bananas.** The highly developed **fruit trade** of Bremen has large storage sheds in the Free Port Dock I at its disposal. These sheds, which mainly serve the traffic of the Bremer Frucht-Handelsgesellschaft, are adapted to the special requirements of the trade in sub-tropical fruit

The storage sheds are able to hold 120 000 t of potash valued at 3 million dollars. "Scrapers" are removing the hardened potash to the conveyor belts.

West Indian bananas are transferred at Bremerhaven to the Scandinavian countries.

(lemons, oranges, grapes, tomatoes, bananas from the Canary Islands, apples, etc.). Steam heating systems protect the fruit from frost.

The steadily increasing import of West Indian bananas to Central Europe during recent years necessitated the erection of special facilities in the Port of Bremerhaven for the rapid discharge of fruit steamers arriving from Central America, and for the speedy transfer of the fruit to its destination. Upon the wide quay on the west side of Kaiser Dock III a covered loading platform with extensive railway sidings and four portable conveyors was built. The latter are set to work simultaneously on the four hatchways of the banana steamers. The hoists which reach with one end close above the bottom of the holds, haul the bunches of bananas in canvas sheets on to the conveyors running alongside the railway fruit cars. Special devices reload part of the fruit cargo into smaller ocean vessels bound for Denmark and the countries of Scandinavia.

West Indian bananas are mechanically discharged for further transport to Central European countries.

Bremen as a passenger port

Bremen has long since been the great German transoceanic passenger port. By the construction of farflung new docks at Bremerhaven the port has kept abreast of the growing demands exercised by the giant liners and the speed records of modern transoceanic traffic. Even the large liners of the type of the Bremen, the Europa and the Columbus may moor directly at the river embankment independent of the tides, since the 3280 ft. long Columbus Quay, built a few years ago, boasts a water-depth of 40 ft. at low tide. Passengers disembarking at Columbus Quay may enter directly the Continental express trains which await them in the Columbus Station, the Station by the Sea. In the closest vicinity lies the local Airport which affords immediate command of special aeroplanes to all parts of Europe. The construction of the titanic North Lock, the world's second-largest lock, is nearing completion. The simultaneous enlargement of one of the dry-docks, the Kaiser Dock II, to a length of 1060 ft. will give docking opportunity to the largest trans-Atlantic liners, while the new lock will permit them a safe passage into the protected inner basins.

The Columbus Quay in Bremerhaven enables even the largest passenger steamers to berth independent of the tides.

Passengers disembarking from liners change directly to the continental express trains at the seaside station on the Columbus Pier

THE DOCKS OF BREMERHAVEN

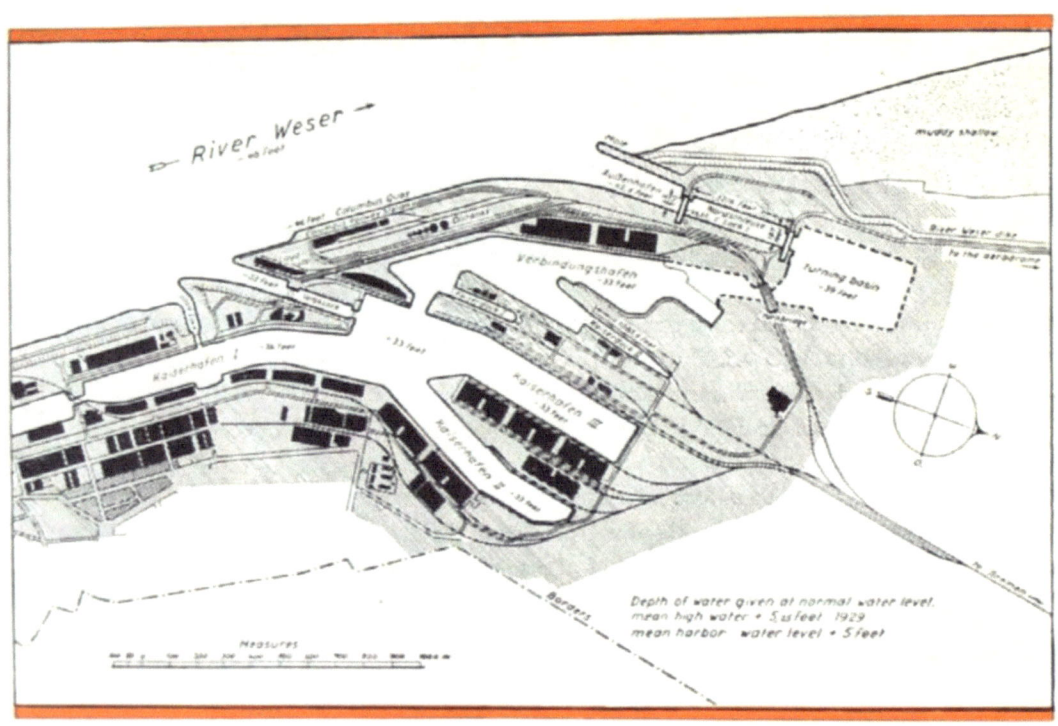

Kaiser Docks I, II and III.	Loading & discharging facilities for ships of all sizes. 11 Quay Sheds. Cotton Sheds.
Transfer of Bananas.	Transfer of West Indian bananas to Central Europe and Scandinavia.
Kaiser Docks I & II.	Dry-docks for vessels up to 1085 ft. long. Repair shops.
Columbus Station.	Pier Station. Express steamers despatched independent of tides.
Oil Bunkering.	Bunkering of largest liners. Maximum capacity 6000 t in 7 hours.
North Lock.	Accessible to super-liners. Entrance width 147.5 ft., length of chamber 1216 ft.

THE DOCKS OF BREMEN-CITY

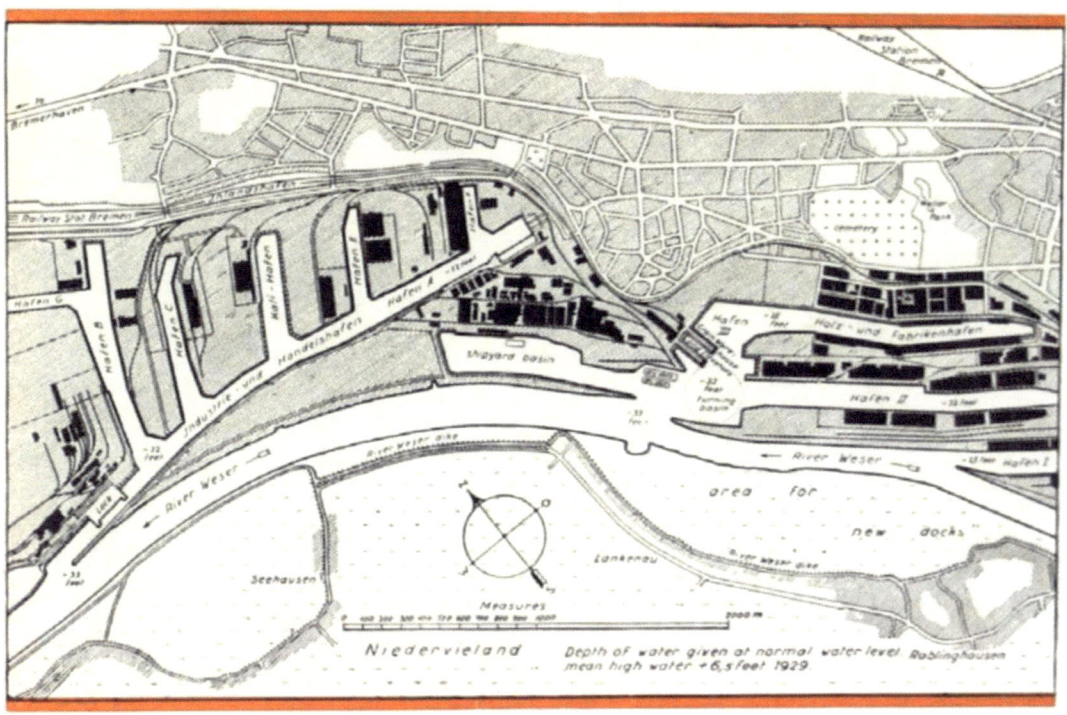

Free Port I.	European oversea traffic. Sheds and warehouses for piece goods, wine, fruit
Free Port II.	Transoceanic traffic. 4 parallel sidings on quays, 14 luffing cranes per ship. Special facilities for the transfer of cotton. Import from all transoceanic countries.
Lumber and Factory Dock.	Grain and oil mills. "Hag" Coffee Works. Cotton stores. Import and treatment of Nordic lumber
Grain Silos.	Mechanical transfer to and from deep-water ship, railway, barge store and cart
Potash Port.	Mechanical transfer to and from store, railway, barge and steamer, loose or in bags.
Industrial and Commercial Dock.	Entered by locks. Iron, lumber and oil industries. Transfer of bulk goods Import of cattle.

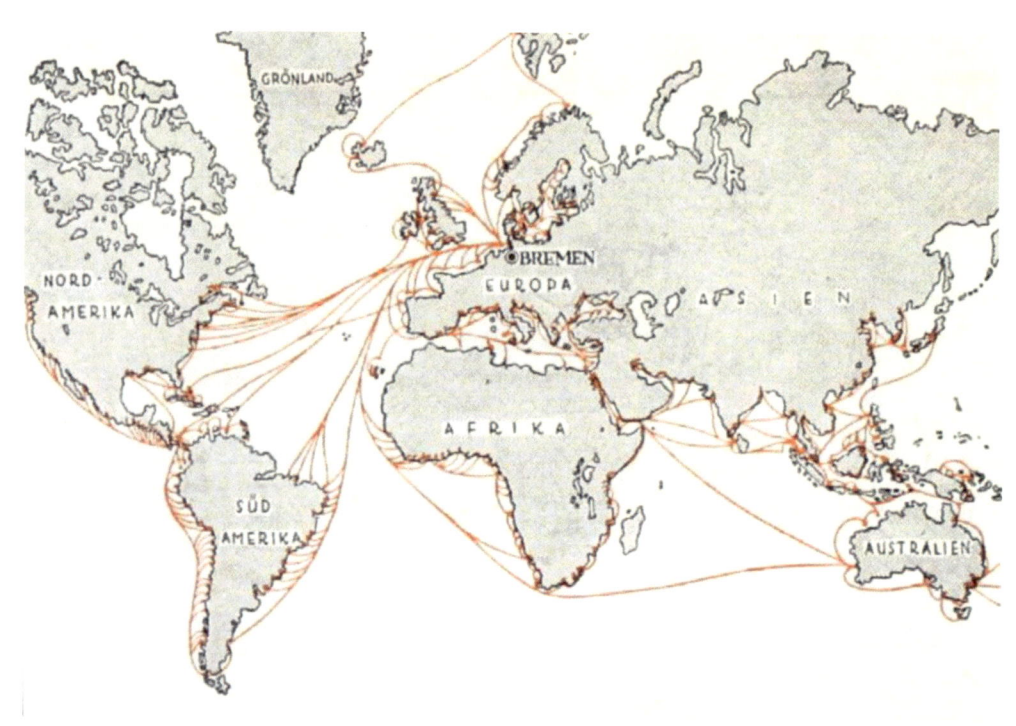

THE NETWORK
OF REGULAR STEAMSHIP LINES STARTING
FROM BREMEN SPANS THE WHOLE GLOBE.